REAL ESTATE MADE SIMPLE

Unlocking the Insider
Secrets the Pros Use to
Buy, Rent, and Flip With
Confidence

STEPHANIE WILLIAMS, MBA

Real Estate Made Simple

Published by Booked and Branded Publishing

www.bookedandbrandedpublishing.com

ISBN: 978-1-969369-10-0

Printed in the United States of America

Dedication

To every first-timer stepping into real estate's vast world—
bold enough to seek the secrets most never hear.

You're not just buying a property; you're unlocking doors
to freedom, wealth, and legacy. This journey can be
challenging, but you're not alone—we're in this together.

The truths shared here are the pro secrets that turn
confusion into clarity, hesitation into confidence. With
every page, I'll be your guide, your teammate, and your
biggest cheerleader.

Here's to you—ready to discover, ready to win, prepared to
build your empire.

Table of Contents

About the Author

Stephanie Williams, MBA, is a strategic business consultant, accomplished entrepreneur, and seasoned real estate investor and mentor with over a decade of proven success across multiple real estate sectors. For the past 10 years, Stephanie has balanced a thriving career in corporate America with building a diverse real estate portfolio that includes personal residences, long-term rentals, Airbnb properties, and profitable flips.

She holds an MBA with a concentration in entrepreneurship from a top-tier program, where she graduated with a perfect GPA, blending academic excellence with sharp business acumen. Stephanie's professional background spans strategic consulting and corporate leadership roles, where she refined her skills in negotiation, financial planning, and operational efficiency—skills she translates to real estate investing.

Passionate about empowering others, Stephanie has guided countless new and seasoned investors through the complexities of property acquisition, financing, negotiation, and management, helping them build sustainable, profitable portfolios. Her coaching emphasizes clarity, confidence, and customized strategies that align with each client's unique goals.

Stephanie is the founder of Booked and Branded Publishing, a premium ghostwriting and consulting firm that supports entrepreneurs and professionals in sharing their expertise and growing their businesses. She combines her deep knowledge of real estate with a strategic mindset to deliver unmatched value and insight.

Her motto—Where hustle meets strategy—reflects her commitment to blending relentless drive with smart, intentional action. Stephanie lives to help others turn dreams into a legacy through education, mentorship, and authentic partnership.

Introduction

Welcome to your real estate journey.

Whether you're reading this as a first-time buyer, a budding investor, or someone seeking to expand an existing portfolio, you've made a powerful choice to take control of your financial future.

Real estate is more than just property—it's a vehicle for freedom, legacy, and wealth creation. Yet, it can also seem intricate and frightening, especially when you're starting. This book is your trusted guide—breaking down the jargon, unveiling insider secrets, and providing practical, actionable steps that you can apply.

Over the past decade, I've built a diverse real estate portfolio while balancing a demanding career in corporate America. Through experience and education, I've learned that success comes not just from knowledge, but from strategy, mindset, and taking consistent, confident action.

Inside these pages, you'll find a roadmap tailored to help you:

- Understand the essential foundations of buying, renting, and flipping
- Navigate financing options that fit your unique situation
- Discover how to find the right properties and negotiate
- Manage your investments for long-term growth
- Cultivate the mindset that fuels persistence and resilience

This is more than a book—it's a partnership. Consider me your mentor, cheerleader, and strategic partner as you embark on this transformative journey.

Every expert investor started somewhere. The difference is that they took that first step and kept going. Now, it's your turn.

Let's get started.

Booked & Branded Publishing

CHAPTER 1

Real Estate Basics for New Buyers and Investors

Welcome. You've just taken the first—and perhaps the most important—step into a world where wealth is not only created but multiplied. Real estate is not just about buying homes or collecting rent checks. It is about shaping your future, crafting opportunities that compound while you sleep, and building a legacy that your family, community, and heirs will benefit from long after you're gone.

Whether you're here to purchase your very first home, secure rental income to free yourself from the limitations of a paycheck, or flip properties for sped-up profits, this chapter lays your foundation. The wealthy know this: **you cannot scale without a firm base.** And that begins with understanding the fundamentals—because in real estate, the basics are never bare. They are the blueprints of empires.

Understanding Property Types Like an Insider

Every investor, no matter how experienced, must master the language of property types. Each type carries its own opportunities, risks, and wealth-building potential. This is not about memorizing definitions; it's about **choosing the right vehicle for your financial strategy.**

1. Primary Residence: The Cornerstone Asset

Your first home is not just where you live. It's often your first significant wealth-building asset. While many see it as just "a place to stay," successful investors know it doubles as a **financial springboard.**

- **Equity Growth:** Every payment you make chips away at debt and builds ownership.
- **Leverage:** Equity can be borrowed against for future investments.
- **Stability:** A residence shields you from volatile rental markets.

Mini Case Example: Marissa purchased her first home in an up-and-coming neighborhood for $210,000. She lived there for five years while working her 9-to-5 job. By the time she sold, that same home was worth $320,000. Without trying, she built $110,000 in equity—equity she later rolled into two cash-flowing rental properties. Her primary residence became her stepping stone into true investment territory.

2. Rental Properties: The Freedom Builder

Rental properties, whether long-term leases or short-term rentals like Airbnb, are where many investors find their path to financial freedom.

- **Long-term Rentals:** provide consistent, predictable cash flow. Think steady checks that help pay off your mortgage and create surplus income.
- **Short-Term Rentals (Airbnb, Vrbo):** Offer higher margins and flexibility. These can often double or triple the returns of traditional rentals—but they demand active management, hospitality skills, and technology know-how.

Insider Note: Properties near hospitals, universities, or tourist districts often outperform the market. Why? Because demand is accounted for in the location.

3. Flips: Accelerated Wealth — If You Do It Right

Flipping is often glamorized on television, but behind the scenes, it's one of the most demanding strategies. Done correctly, flipping can transform capital. Done incorrectly, it can drain reserves just as fast.

- The goal: immediate understanding.
- Potential dangers encompass: substantial preliminary expenses. The schedule was rigid. Reliance on the ebb and flow of the market.
- Buying right, precise budgeting, and strategic selling: that's the secret to success.

Mini Case Example: Derrick bought a distressed property for $140,000, invested $45,000 in innovative renovations (new kitchen, upgraded bathrooms, curb appeal), and resold it for $260,000 within 90 days—his net profit: $55,000. But here's the key—he had multiple contractor quotes, a timeline he stuck to, and a realtor who specialized in flips. Without that, his margins could have collapsed.

4. Commercial & Land: The Legacy Plays

This is where advanced investors operate—shopping centers, apartment buildings, raw land near growth corridors. These plays require higher capital and expertise, but they also offer higher returns and long-term stability.

- **Commercial properties:** Provide diversified income streams through multiple tenants.
- **Land investments:** Strategic land purchases near highways, airports, or development zones can be appreciated.

This is often the space where investors transition from "side hustlers" to **empire builders.**

Pro Secret

Successful investors don't dabble. They choose their lane, master it, and then expand. The fastest way to lose money in real estate is to chase every shiny opportunity for understanding which path aligns with your resources, skills, and goals.

Pro Tip

If you're starting out, don't be seduced by the "fast money" appeal of flipping or commercial deals. Start with a property type that matches your spare capacity, risk tolerance, and financial runway. The right deal at the right stage of your journey will create momentum that lasts.

Quick Knowledge Check

Which of these property types is considered more hands-on and at higher risk?

A) Primary Residence
B) Rental Property
C) Flip
D) Commercial Property

Answer: C) Flip — Because flipping involves renovations, strict timelines, and rapid resale, it demands active management, upfront capital, and exposes you to higher risks than other entry-level property types.

Why Location Still Rules?

You've heard it before—and you'll hear it again: **location drives everything.** A substantial property in the wrong area will underperform, while a modest property in a thriving neighborhood can become a goldmine.

- **Appreciation:** areas with strong job markets, excellent schools, and growing infrastructure will increase in value faster.
- **Resale Potential:** A property in a prime location sells and commands higher prices.
- **Rental Demand:** Tenants want safety, convenience, and accessibility. Properties near hospitals, universities, or transit hubs sit vacant.
- **Quality of Life:** If you're buying a primary residence, consider how the location affects your daily routines, access to services, and lifestyle.

Case Example: In 2021, I purchased an older townhouse just six minutes from the Atlanta Airport. The purchase price was $160,000. Today, it's valued at around $240,000, and newer homes in the same area sell for $300,000+. Why? The neighborhood was strengthening because of new highways, commercial developments, and increased demand. **Location transformed the property's future, not the property itself.**

Real Estate Lingo You Must Master

Before you proceed further, commit these terms to memory—they are the language of wealth builders:

- **Equity:** The portion of property you own after debts.
- **Appreciation:** the increase in property value.
- **Cash flow:** rental income minus expenses. Positive cash flow = profit.
- **Cap Rate:** The return measure investors use to evaluate rentals.
- **Loan-to-Value (LTV):** The ratio of loan amount to property value.
- **Contingency:** Conditions (like inspections or financing) that must be met before closing.

Define your goal, because this shapes everything

Why are you investing? To live, to rent, to flip, or to hold long-term? Your **"why"** determines your **"how."**

- A primary residence builds stability and foundational wealth.
- Rentals create freedom through passive income.
- Flips speed up cash for reinvestment.

Commercial and land investments create generational wealth.

Gentle Reflection

Pause here. Ask yourself:

- Are you craving stability or speed?
- What do you prefer, long-term wealth or short-term wins?
- Does your real estate support your lifestyle or define your legacy?

Write your primary goal. Hold it close. This clarity will guide you not only through this book but also sharpen your decisions for years to come.

CHAPTER 2

Financing Made Friendly —
Your Proper Path to Property Ownership

F inancing is often the most intimidating part of real estate for new buyers and investors. Numbers, banks, paperwork—it can feel like a maze. But here's the truth: financing is not about fear; it's about strategy. Once you understand how lenders think, you'll see loans not as obstacles but as **powerful tools for leverage**. The right financing doesn't just buy you property; it speeds up your path to wealth and legacy.

Think of financing as the **bridge** between where you are today and the property you want tomorrow. The stronger and smarter your bridge, the smoother your journey will be.

Your Credit Score: The Silent Gatekeeper

Your credit score is one of the first things lenders see. To them, it's your financial reputation in a single number. A high score whispers, "This borrower is trustworthy." A low score raises doubts.

I remember when I first began focusing on my credit—it wasn't stellar. But with consistent effort and discipline, I raised my score to 830. That single shift unlocked financing options I had never imagined. My interest rates plummeted. Loan approvals came more easily. Over time, those lower payments saved me **tens of thousands of dollars**—money I could reinvest into properties instead of handing over to the bank.

Story: The 90-Day Turnaround Take Jasmine, a client of mine. She came to me with a 610 score—too low for most competitive loans. Within 90 days, she followed a structured plan: disputing errors on her report, paying down high-interest cards, and setting up automatic payments. By the end of three months, her score jumped to 685. That single change dropped her mortgage interest rate by 1%. Over the life of her loan, that improvement saved her **$38,000**. Financing mastery isn't about perfection—it's about progress.

Pro Secret

Lenders pull your score from the three major bureaus—Experian, Equifax, and TransUnion. Here's the catch: they often use your middle score—not your highest or lowest. Raise the middle number, and your options multiply.

Pro Tip

Check your credit reports for free at AnnualCreditReport. com. Look for mistakes and fix them before applying. For ongoing monitoring, use tools like Credit Karma or paid services from your bank. Information is power.

Insider Financing Options You Should Know

Most buyers only hear about conventional or FHA loans. But wealthy investors? They are aware of **creative financing vehicles** that most people overlook. Here are a few:

- **Navy Federal's HomeBuyer's Choice Program**—A valid zero-down option for eligible military members and their families, with no PMI required. That's thousands saved upfront.
- **Investor-Friendly "No-Doc" Loans**—Perfect for self-employed professionals, freelancers, or full-time investors. Lenders like Lima One Capital and CoreVest verify income using bank statements or assets rather than W-2s.
- **Portfolio Loans**—Some community banks keep loans "in-house," offering flexible underwriting standards for strong local borrowers.

Story: The Freelancer's Breakthrough. Aaron was a graphic designer with inconsistent paychecks. Traditional banks rejected him. But with a no-doc loan based on his business deposits, he bought a duplex, lived in one unit, and rented the other. Three years later, that property became his springboard to three more acquisitions. What banks saw as "unstable," an investor-friendly lender saw as potential.

Understanding Interest Rates

Interest rates are the **price tag of money.** Even a slight difference—say, 0.25%—can save or cost you tens of thousands.

- **Fixed-Rate Mortgages**—Predictability for 15–30 years. Ideal if you plan to hold long term.
- **Adjustable-Rate Mortgages (ARMs)**–Lower rates upfront, with adjustments later. Great, if you plan to sell or refinance before the change. Risky if you stay longer.
- **Factors That Shape Rates**–Your credit score, down payment size, loan program, and even market conditions.

Luxury Insight: High-net-worth investors often negotiate rate burdens by offering larger deposits or purchasing points. These strategies reduce long-term costs.

Pro Tip

Never accept the first rate offered. Shop around. And if rates are rising, ask about "locking in" before your approval expires. This is the difference between average financing and elite financing.

The Big Five Financing Options

- **Conventional Loans**–Great for borrowers with strong credit.
- **FHA Loans–lower** down payments (as little as 3.5%) - designed for accessibility.
- **VA Loans**–Exclusive to veterans and active-duty service members. Often zero down.
- **USDA Loans–for** rural or semi-rural homes. Zero down if eligible.
- **Hard money loans**–short-term financing, ideal for flippers who need speed.

And of course, the **cash purchase**—rare but powerful. Nothing beats walking into a deal with full liquidity.

Down Payments & PMI

The famous "20% down" rule is not mandatory. With the FHA, VA, or USDA, you can start with less. The trade-off? **PMI (private mortgage insurance).** It adds cost to your payment, but here's the mindset shift: PMI is not a penalty; it's a stepping stone. It gets you into the market faster, so your property can appreciate today.

Preparing Your Loan Application Like a Pro

Applying for a mortgage is like preparing for a job interview. Come ready.

Gather:

- Pay stubs
- Tax returns
- Bank statements
- Proof of assets

Lenders will also analyze your **debt-to-income ratio (DTI)**—under 43%. Elite borrowers aim lower, which signals strength.

Creative Financing Hacks in Competitive Markets

When traditional loans aren't enough, sophisticated investors pull out alternative strategies:

- **Seller Financing**–Cut out the bank and pay the seller. Faster closings, creative terms.
- **Lease Option Agreements**–Rent now, buy later. A powerful way to control property today.
- **Private Money Partnerships**–Partner with individuals seeking steady returns.
- **HELOCs (Home Equity Line of Credit)**–use existing equity as leverage for your subsequent acquisition.

Story: The Power of Partnerships Maya didn't have enough for a down payment on a fourplex, but her uncle had idle capital. Together, they structured a private money deal—he funded 50% for a fixed return, and she managed everything.

Three years later, the property's appreciation and cash flow had more than doubled his investment. He got reliable returns, and she grew her portfolio without waiting years to save.

Pro Tip: The Quiet Wealth
Add even $100 extra to your payment, and you'll shave years off a 30-year loan. Over time, this "quiet wealth builder" can save tens of thousands in interest.

Knowledge Check

What credit score do you need to qualify for a conventional loan?

A) 450   B) 620   C) 700   D) 800

Answer: B) 620 — Most conventional loans require a minimum of 620. But the higher your score, the better your terms. At 740+, you unlock elite-level financing.

Gentle Reflection

Pause and breathe. Financing is not about fear—it's about freedom. Ask yourself:

- What's the one thing holding me back from applying?
- Do I need to improve my score, save for a down payment, or get pre-approved?

- What steps can I take **this week** to move closer to ownership?

Please write it down. Commit to it. Every step, no matter how small, builds the bridge to your legacy.

CHAPTER 3

The Right of Property —
Your Clever Search Guide

N ow that you've secured financing, the next phase begins: **finding the property that matches your goals, your lifestyle, and your long-term wealth strategy.** This is where many new investors make mistakes. They fall in love with appearances or chase "cheap" deals without understanding the deeper forces that drive property success.

Think of this stage as a **luxury treasure hunt.** Your financing is the map, but the "X" that marks the spot depends on how skillfully you evaluate **location, condition, and timing.** Choose here, and you don't just buy a property; position yourself to build a legacy.

Why Location Is the Kingmaker?

You've heard it before: *location, location, location.* But let's elevate that: location isn't just important—it's the single most significant driver of long-term appreciation, rental demand, and resale potential.

Here's why:

- **Appreciation—properties** near strong job markets, reputable schools, and expanding infrastructure grow faster in value. Consider what happened in Austin, Texas. Investors who bought modest homes near the burgeoning tech corridor a decade ago have now seen values triple—because the job market transformed the area.
- **Resale Potential**—Life changes. Careers shift. Families grow. When it's time to sell, a property in a desirable location gives you leverage. Buyers compete for well-placed homes, often driving prices above asking.
- **Rental Demand**—Tenants gravitate toward convenience and safety. Proximity to universities, hospitals, transit, and retail hubs keeps vacancy low and cash flow steady.
- **Quality of Life**—If you're buying for yourself, location defines your daily comfort. Commutes, grocery runs, access to healthcare, and lifestyle amenities shape not just convenience but happiness—and by extension, future property value.

Pro Tip

If you're buying for your family, research schools even if you don't have children. School quality drives value. Properties in top-rated districts outperform because families will always prioritize education.

Pro Secret: The Airport Townhouse

In 2021, I purchased an older townhouse near the Atlanta airport. It wasn't glamorous, but the location was prime: six minutes from the airport, with new highways and commercial developments planned. I paid $160,000. Within three years, it was appraised at $240,000—and the built homes nearby sold for $300,000+. My gain wasn't about granite countertops or luxury finishes—it was about the perfect combination of location and timing.

The Hidden Advantage of Micro-Markets

Most investors stop at the ZIP code level. The wealthy go deeper.

A **micro-market** is a hyper-local pocket where trends shift faster than city averages. Two blocks can mean different appreciation curves, tenant profiles, or rental rates.

Here's what to study:

- **School Ratings**–Within the same district, a single boundary line can mean a $50,000–$100,000 difference in home value.
- **Infrastructure Projects**–A planned train stop or new retail plaza can boost nearby values years before most buyers notice.
- **Walkability & Lifestyle Stores**—Millennials and Gen Z renters pay premiums for properties within walking distance to coffee shops, parks, and gyms.
- **Community Insights**–Join local Facebook or Nextdoor groups. Residents often reveal insider

details: future developments, zoning changes, or even cultural shifts that don't yet appear in public reports.

Story: The Coffee Shop Effect. One of my clients purchased a duplex on a quiet street. It seemed average. Six months later, a trendy cafe and co-working space opened a block away. Young professionals flooded the area, rental demand soared, and his units leased at 20% above projected rent. One coffee shop turned its "average" property into a high-demand asset.

Timing the Market Like a Professional

Real estate isn't just about what you buy—it's about **when you buy.** Markets move in cycles.

- **Buyer's Market**–High inventory, low demand. Negotiation power is on your side.
- **Seller's Market**–Low inventory, high demand. Prices climb, competition intensifies.

Neither market is "good" nor "bad." They require different strategies. In a buyer's market, you negotiate. In a seller's market, you must move and often rely on creative financing to stand out.

Luxury Insight

Elite investors monitor leading indicators—like building permits filed, job growth stats, and rental absorption rates—rather than waiting for headlines. By the time the media announces a "hot market," the best investors are already three steps ahead.

Tools & Experts That Give You the Edge

The right property isn't found by luck. It's identified with strategy and the right allies.

- **MLS Access**–Work with an agent who can pull real-time MLS data. Online platforms (Zillow, Redfin, Realtor.com) are helpful, but they lag professional databases.
- **Expert Agents**—Don't settle for a generalist. Align with an agent who understands investment goals and micro-markets. They should bring you deals, not just open doors.
- **Inspectors & Appraisers**–Always vet beyond the surface. A polished exterior can hide costly plumbing, foundation, or roofing issues.
- **Title companies**–elite investors never skip title searches. A clouded title or unpaid lien can turn a dream purchase into a nightmare.

Story: The Hidden Foundation A first-time buyer once told me she closed on a charming bungalow until her inspector uncovered severe foundation issues—repairs that would have cost $50,000. That inspection saved her from financial ruin. She redirected her financing to a duplex that is now one of her best-performing rentals.

Red Flags to Recognize

Not every attractive property is a wise investment. Watch for:

- Homes that linger unsold for months without reason.
- Sudden, unexplained price drops.
- Signs of neglect: leaking roofs, cracked foundations, outdated electrical systems.
- Title issues, liens, or unclear ownership histories.

Sometimes, the most intelligent decision is not to buy. Walking away preserves your capital for the right opportunity.

Knowledge Check

Question: Name two key factors to research about a property's location.

Answer: Job market strength and school quality. Bonus: safety, amenities, and planned developments also impact value.

Gentle Reflection

Close your eyes and imagine where you'd like to build your legacy. Is it a vibrant city with endless energy? A serene suburb where families thrive? Or perhaps a developing town poised for growth?

Now, write **three non-negotiables** for your ideal location—whether it's commute time, school district quality, or rental demand. These will be your compass, helping you stay focused as you sift through the noise and discover your ideal property.

CHAPTER 4

The Right of Property —

Strategies & Instruments to Succeed

By now, you've clarified your financing options and identified the type of property that matches your goals. Now comes the pivotal step: **entering the marketplace with precision.** This is where theory transforms into action. Deals are made or missed in this phase, and your ability to navigate timing, tools, and trusted experts will separate you from the average buyer.

Think of this chapter as your **investment armor.** Every strategy here helps you move not just—but—so you secure opportunities that others overlook.

Market Timing: Knowing When to Strike

Real estate is cyclical, but those cycles are not random. Understanding them allows you to time your entry like a seasoned investor.

- **Buyer's Market**–Inventory is high, demand is low. You hold the leverage. This is where you negotiate repairs, demand credits, and push for aggressive discounts. The wise investor collects properties at below-market value while others hesitate.
- **The competition is high, and there's not much available.** Multiple offers become the norm. To win, you must move with speed, craft stronger offers, and sometimes include creative terms that outshine competitors.

Neither phase is "good" or "bad." The wealthy know how to thrive in both.

Tracking the Market Like an Insider

- Review **local Realtor association reports** for month-to-month shifts.
- Watch dashboards like **Redfin Data Center** or **Zillow Research** for trends in price per square foot, days on market, and list-to-sale ratios.
- Study **neighborhood-level sales**, not just city averages. Hyper-local insights tell the true story.

Pro Secret

Set up instant MLS alerts that match your criteria. In a fast-moving seller's market, being the *first* to act can be the difference between securing a cash-flowing rental and losing it to a competitor.

Virtual Tours and Open Houses: Merging Tech with Tact

The digital era has changed property searches forever. Today, an investor can tour homes from across the country in minutes. Though technology is a powerful tool, there's no substitute for seeing the land with your own eyes.

- **Virtual Tours**–Use 3D walkthroughs, aerial drone footage, and video tours to pre-screen properties. This saves time and narrows the focus.
- **Open Houses**–Nothing replaces the energy of being inside a property. You see how light hits the rooms, hear neighborhood sounds, and even notice subtle details like traffic flow or street activity.

Pro Tip

Bring a simple rating system to every showing. Score properties 1–5 on factors like layout, location, condition, and investment potential. After five showings, details blur. Your notes will protect you from making emotional, impulsive decisions.

Investor Story: The Sunlight Deal One of my clients passed on a triplex because the online photos looked dark and dated. But at the open house, morning sunlight poured into the units, transforming the space. He purchased it, staged it, and the natural light became its biggest rental appeal. Virtual tools help—but in-person vision closes deals.

Working with Real Estate Agents: Building Your Power Team

Your real estate agent is not just a "door opener." They are your strategist, connector, and negotiator. The right agent can make or break your investment outcomes.

Look for agents who:

- Have **local expertise** in your chosen micro-markets.
- **Listen first, talk second**—they must understand *your* goals, not just push listings.
- Demonstrate a track record of **winning negotiations** and working with investors.

Example: The Off-Market Advantage. I once partnered with an agent who specialized in investment properties. She didn't just show listings—she brought me off-market deals, introduced me to a property manager, and even flagged landlord-friendly zoning laws. That relationship alone generated thousands in savings and faster tenant placements. A potent agent isn't an expense—it's a wealth multiplier.

Home Inspections: Your Due Diligence Shield

Inspections are not optional. They serve as your defense against purchasing a liability disguised as an opportunity.
Inspectors evaluate:

- Structural integrity: roof, foundation, framing.
- Mechanical systems: plumbing, electrical, HVAC.
- Safety hazards: mold, asbestos, radon.

A $500 inspection today could save you from a $15,000 repair tomorrow.

Pro Secret
Always include an inspection contingency in your offer. This gives you legal leverage to renegotiate or walk away if issues surface.

Pro Tip
Attend the inspection in person. Seeing the cracks in the foundation or rust in the HVAC system firsthand equips you with authority when renegotiating. Inspectors often share maintenance tips that save you money long-term—wisdom you miss if you only read the report.

Case Study: The $40K Save. A client once fell in love with an artisan-style home. On the surface, it looked flawless. During inspection, however, a hidden drainage issue was uncovered that would have cost $40,000 in long-term damage. Because of the contingency, the seller credited the repair costs back at closing. Without that inspection, it would have been a financial disaster.

Appraisers & Title Companies: Quiet Protectors of Your Wealth

Behind every safe transaction are these two professionals:

- **Appraisers–they** confirm the property's market value. This protects you from overpaying and ensures the bank funds your loan.
- **Title companies–**they safeguard your ownership rights. Title professionals dig into records to uncover liens, disputes, or ownership challenges. Skipping this step risks inheriting legal battles you didn't create.

Investor Note: A luxury client once attempted to purchase a vacation home without a title search. The property later revealed unpaid contractor liens. Had the sale closed, he would have inherited a six-figure problem. That $700 title fee saved him a potential $100,000 loss.

Warning Signs: Properties to Walk Away From

Not every listing deserves your attention. Recognize red flags early:

- Homes that sit unsold for months without an obvious reason.
- Sellers are urging you to "skip the inspection."
- Disclosures that are incomplete or vague.
- Complicated or unclear ownership history.

Remember: walking away is not weakness—it's strength. Protecting your capital today ensures you're ready for the right opportunity tomorrow.

Knowledge Check

Question: What's one key benefit of hiring a local real estate agent?

Answer: Local agents bring deep market knowledge, access to off-market listings, and negotiation skills that maximize your deal potential.

Gentle Reflection

Picture yourself walking through your ideal investment property. Sunlight floods the living room. The floor creaks with history. You can already envision tenants signing leases or your family gathering for dinner.

Ask yourself: **What matters most in a property for me?** Is it long-term cash flow? Family comfort? Future resale? Write your top three must-haves. These will anchor you when emotions run high and keep you focused on building a portfolio that supports your legacy.

CHAPTER 5

Negotiation Strategies That Work

Negotiation in real estate is often misunderstood. Too many buyers believe it's about pushing for the lowest possible price. But true professionals know that **negotiation is the art of creating agreements where both parties walk away satisfied.** It's not war; it's a puzzle. The more pieces you understand — price, timing, terms, motivation, relationships — the easier it is to assemble a picture that works to your advantage.

When you master the strategies below, you don't just "save a little money." You secure deals others thought impossible, turn hidden problems into financial wins, and move forward with confidence that your wealth is being built, not by chance.

Know Your Market Power

Before drafting an offer, you must understand the climate you're operating in. Negotiating without context is like walking into a boxing match blindfolded.

- **Buyer's Market (More Supply Than Demand)** This is your arena of leverage. Sellers compete for your attention, which means you can negotiate repairs, request seller-paid closing costs, or press for price reductions. They need you more than you need them.

- **Seller's Market (More Demand Than Supply)** This is the opposite battlefield. Homes sell, often above asking price. Price flexibility shrinks, but that doesn't mean you can't negotiate. Here, terms matter as much as dollars. Flexible timing, clean contracts, or even a slight personal touch can tilt the decision in your favor.

Pro Secret

Many buyers focus on lowering the purchase price. But a $5,000 reduction may save you only a few dollars on your monthly payment. A $5,000 seller credit toward closing costs slashes the cash you need upfront — a massive benefit if liquidity is tight. High-level negotiators don't just chase price; they optimize the entire structure of the deal.

Build Rapport: Relationships Close Deals

Never forget: real estate is not a numbers-only game. It is human. Sellers are attached to their homes. Agents are protecting their reputations. Emotions influence decisions more than most people realize.

That's why negotiations conducted with warmth, professionalism, and respect often outperform aggressive tactics. A seller may accept your offer, even if it's not the highest, because they feel you'll honor their home.

Keys to Building Rapport

- **Be personable.** Where allowed, include a buyer's letter. A brief note about why you love the property or how you envision living there creates a bond.
- **Stay professional.** Politeness and respect set you apart in a field where too many buyers treat negotiations as combat.
- **Ask open-ended questions.** "What's most important to you in this sale — timing, price, or certainty of closing?" Often, the answer reveals the true lever.

Pro Tip

If the seller needs a quick close, offer to expedite inspections and financing. If they need time to move, grant flexibility on possession. These "non-financial wins" often carry more weight than squeezing out a few extra dollars.

Story: The 10-Day Close One of my clients landed a coveted duplex in a heated seller's market without offering the highest bid. How? The seller needed certainty and speed. By promising a 10-day close and waiving unnecessary contingencies, we beat out three higher offers. That's the power of aligning with what the seller values most.

Key Negotiation Tactics

Here are tested strategies used by top-tier investors:

- **Negotiate Repairs as Credits**–After inspection, request credits instead of asking the seller to fix issues. This gives you control over repair quality and often saves money.
- **Flex on Timing**–Offer flexible closing dates. Sometimes, a month of extra move-out time is worth more to a seller than an additional $10,000.
- **Use Contingencies**–Inspection, appraisal, and financing contingencies protect you. But don't overload your offer with too many, or you'll weaken your position. Balance safety with competitiveness.
- **Leverage Market Knowledge**–If a property has been sitting on the market for months, highlight that in negotiations. If it's a hot listing, make your offer shine with strong terms.
- **Primary Silence**–State your request and stop talking. The silence often pressures the seller to respond — or concede. Too many buyers sabotage themselves by filling the silence with unnecessary concessions.

- **Be Willing to Walk Away**–The strongest position in negotiation is the ability to say, "No deal." There will always be another property. Fear of missing out has cost more investors than bad market timing ever did.

Case Study: The $12K Roof. In one of my earliest deals, the inspection revealed roof issues estimated at $12,000. Instead of panicking or walking, I requested an $8,000 seller credit. They agreed, eager to close. After closing, I hired my contractor, who fixed the issue for $7,500 — leaving me with $500 extra in my pocket. Negotiation turned a liability into profit.

Contracts: Put Every Agreement in Writing

A handshake does not weigh real estate. If it's not written, it doesn't exist. Protect yourself by ensuring **every term you negotiate is captured in the purchase contract.**

- Seller credits
- Agreed repairs
- Contingencies
- Timelines

Think of your contract as your **shield**. It enforces clarity, accountability, and professionalism — and it ensures that emotions or misunderstandings never derail the deal.

Common Mistakes to Avoid

Even seasoned buyers stumble here. Avoid these traps:

- **Falling in love with one property.** Emotional attachment clouds judgment. Always have a Plan B.
- **Focusing only on price.** Terms, timing, and conditions can carry equal — or greater — weight.
- **Over-negotiating.** Push too hard and the deal dies. Try to find solutions that benefit everyone, not just yourself.
- **Skipping inspection credits.** Even minor issues can be leveraged into meaningful savings.

Knowledge Check

Question: Name two negotiation tactics that can save you money or stress.
   Answer:

1. Negotiating seller credits toward closing costs to reduce upfront expenses.
2. Offering flexible closing dates to make your offer more attractive without raising the purchase price.

Gentle Reflection

Close your eyes for a moment. Imagine yourself sitting across the table from a seller. You've made your request. Silence hangs in the air. A feeling of calm, composure, and confidence arises. Numbers are known by you, you know. You know your alternatives. You're not desperate — you're deliberate.

That is the essence of powerful negotiation. It's not about aggression. It's about clarity, patience, and strength.

Ask yourself: **What kind of negotiator do I want to become?**

- The buyer who rushes, fears, and overpays?
- Or the investor who listens, adapts, and builds wealth through strategy?

Write one area where you can improve your negotiation style. Perhaps it's practicing patience, asking more questions, or learning to embrace silence. That single shift could save you thousands on your very next deal.

CHAPTER 6

Your Investments: Rentals and Airbnbs

O wning rental properties can be one of the most gratifying—and profitable—paths in real estate. But make no mistake: passive income is never passive without proper systems, strategies, and management. Whether you lean toward the stability of long-term tenants, the flexibility of co-living arrangements, or the fast-paced returns of short-term rentals like Airbnb, your approach must be intentional.

Think of rentals as a business within your business. Your property is the storefront. Your tenants are your customers. And your systems—the way you screen, manage, and optimize—determine whether your rental empire thrives or collapses under stress.

Let's walk through the tools, strategies, and insider methods that will not only protect your investments but elevate them to wealth-building assets.

Tenant Screening Resources for Long-Term Rentals

Tenant screening is your first line of defense. One bad tenant can cost you thousands in unpaid rent, damages, or legal fees. One good tenant can make the next five years effortless. That's why I tell my clients: *screening is not an expense—it's an insurance policy*.

Here are trusted platforms that simplify screening:

- **Zillow Rental Manager** — free online applications and credit/background checks. Easy to use, especially for first-time landlords.
- **Avail** — Free basic screening with affordable upgrades. Includes lease templates and rent tracking—perfect for landlords managing multiple units.
- **TurboTenant** — free rental applications, plus credit and background reports. Useful for independent landlords.
- **TransUnion SmartMove** — affordable, detailed reports from a credit bureau itself. A gold standard in reliability.

Luxury-Level Insight: I once had a tenant application that looked perfect on paper—steady job, high income, spotless references. But SmartMove revealed an eviction from two years earlier that other reports missed. That single check saved me from a $15,000 mistake. Always invest in the deepest screening possible.

Maintenance & Repair Management Tools

Property maintenance is where many landlords burn out. Without systems, minor issues pile up and become major headaches. Professional investors don't wait for fires to start—they build infrastructure to handle them.

- **Buildium** — all-in-one property management software with maintenance request tracking and accounting features.
- **AppFolio** — a robust platform for landlords with multiple properties, offering rent collection, maintenance management, and tenant portals.
- **Maintenance Care** — great for landlords who want to schedule and track repairs in a structured way.

Pro Secret

Encourage tenants to submit repair requests through a single system, not text or email. This ensures everything is documented. A clear paper trail reduces disputes and helps you spot recurring issues early.

Co-living and room rental platforms

If your goal is to maximize rental income, co-living platforms offer a creative path. Instead of renting one unit to one family, you rent rooms to multiple tenants, multiplying cash flow.

- **Nomad**
  - *Pros:* Boosts rental income and reduces vacancy risk by managing leases and helping find tenants.
  - *Cons:* Requires more tenant coordination and oversight.
- **PadSplit**
  - *Pros:* Specializes in affordable, flexible weekly rentals. Ideal for maximizing occupancy.
  - *Cons:* higher turnover and more active management required.

Case Study: The PadSplit Duplex One investor I coached turned a traditional $1,600-per-month duplex into a PadSplit property renting by the room. With six tenants, the same property now generates over $3,200 a month, double the income. Yes, management intensity increased, but with the right system, the return outweighed the hassle.

Housing for Nurses & Traveling Professionals

Healthcare workers, especially travel nurses, are a hidden gem in rental markets. They require **short-term, furnished, reliable housing**, often lasting 3–6 months. Demand is consistent because the tenants are trustworthy.

- **Furnished Finder** — the go-to platform for travel nurse housing.
- **Vivian Health (NurseFly)** — connects healthcare workers with jobs and housing nationwide.

- **Nesterly** — an intergenerational home-sharing platform, often used by healthcare professionals.
- **Roomi** — an app-based service for finding roommates and short-term housing.

Pro Tip

Travel nurses often work with stipends from hospitals, meaning **guaranteed rent** is common. By furnishing a unit, you can command premium rates compared to traditional long-term tenants.

Airbnb & Short-Term Rental Platforms

Short-term rentals (STRs) like Airbnb can be lucrative—but they're not for the faint of heart. They require marketing savvy, operational systems, and attention to detail. But with the right strategy, they can outpace traditional rentals by 2–3x.

- **Airbnb** — the market leader, with built-in protections and a massive global audience.
- **Vrbo** — Best for families and longer-term vacationers.
- **Booking.com** — strong international reach, ideal for urban investors.
- **HomeAway** — part of Vrbo, offering similar benefits with a different traveler base.

Luxury-Level Insight: Treat an Airbnb like a boutique hotel. High-thread-count sheets, thoughtful welcome baskets, and fast response times translate into 5-star reviews, higher nightly rates, and repeat bookings. STR success is not just about location—it's about the guest experience.

Assessing Airbnb Potential Before Buying

Too many investors jump into STRs without analyzing the numbers. Before buying, you must project revenue with data-driven precision.

- **AirDNA** — the gold standard for STR analytics, showing occupancy rates, average daily rates, and revenue projections.
- **Mashvisor** compares Airbnb data against traditional rental performance, helping you decide which strategy fits.
- **Rentometer** benchmarks rental rates in your neighborhood for both long- and short-term stays.

Critical Rule: Always verify local laws first. Many cities have restrictions on STRs—some limit permits, others ban them outright. Never assume your agent will flag this. Research municipal codes before you close.

Knowledge Check

Question: Which of the following tools can help you evaluate Airbnb's potential before purchasing a property?

A) Zillow Rental Manager
B) AirDNA
C) Buildium
D) PadSplit

Answer & Explanation: The correct answer is **B —
AirDNA.** This platform provides occupancy rates, average
daily rates, and revenue projections, making it one of the
most reliable forecasting tools for STR investors.

Gentle Reflection

Pause for a moment. Imagine your ideal rental portfolio. Do
you see yourself with a handful of long-term tenants who
pay on time and treat your property with care? Or do you
see yourself managing high-energy Airbnbs, hosting guests
from around the world? Perhaps you like the creativity of
co-living, maximizing every square foot for income.

Each model is valid—but each demands a different level
of time, energy, and risk tolerance.

Write your answer:

- Long-term stability?
- Short-term flexibility?
- Shared housing cash flow?

Your clarity here will shape your path forward. In real estate,
indecision is costly—but strategy builds legacies.

CHAPTER 7

Flipping Properties Without Losing Your Shirt

F lipping houses has become almost mythologized in real estate. The glossy TV shows, the before-and-after photos, the quick profits—it all looks glamorous. But the truth? Flipping is one of the high-risk, **high-reward** strategies you can pursue. When done correctly, it can deliver life-changing profits in a matter of months. When done, it can drain your capital, your energy, and even your confidence.

The difference between those two outcomes is not luck. It is **planning, discipline, and strategy.**

If you want to flip properties without losing your shirt, you need more than a hammer and vision board. You need numbers that make sense, a team you can trust, and the discipline to walk away from the wrong deals—even if they look tempting.

Let's walk through the essentials that separate seasoned professionals from beginners who burn out.

Step 1: Finding the Right Property — Where Location Meets Potential

You've heard it before: **location is king.** But in flipping, the condition of the property is the queen. They need to work together to win the game.

- **Neighborhood Growth:** Look for areas on the rise. Proximity to transit, new commercial developments, and improving school districts are signs of future demand.
- **Property Type:** Cosmetic fixer-uppers are ideal for beginners. A property that needs only paint, flooring, and updated fixtures offers more predictable profits. Full structural rehabs are better left to seasoned flippers with deep pockets.
- **Red Flags:** Catastrophic damage, foundational issues, or properties with a history of liens and lawsuits can spin a flip into a financial pit.

Mentor Insight: On one of my earliest flips, I walked away from what looked like a great deal because the property sat in a flood zone. Two years later, the area flooded, wiping out dozens of homes. Walking away saved me hundreds of thousands of dollars in potential losses. Sometimes the smartest flip is the one you *don't* do.

Step 2: Running the Numbers — The Flip Budget

Your profit is locked in **the moment you buy, not when you sell.** Overpay at purchase, and no amount of renovation magic will save you.

Here's what to calculate before you write an offer:

- **Purchase Price:** Negotiate hard. Every $1,000 you save here is an extra $1,000 in your pocket later.
- **Renovation Costs:**
  - Always get at least three contractor bids.
  - Use platforms like **Thumbtack, HomeAdvisor, or Angi** to compare vetted professionals.
  - Don't chase the cheapest option; value lies in quality and reliability.
  - Include materials, labor, permits, inspections, and contingencies.
- **Holding Costs:** property taxes, insurance, mortgage payments, and utilities. Every month you hold the property, these eat into your profit.
- **Selling Costs:** Realtor commissions, staging, closing fees, and marketing.
- **Contingency:** Always add 10–20% padding to your budget. Renovations come in under cost.

Pro Secret

I once tried to save money on flooring by using a budget installer. Within six months, buyers complained of warping planks. I had to redo the entire job, doubling my costs. Quality upfront saves money in the long run.

Step 3: Assemble Your Dream Team

Flipping is not a solo sport. It's a team effort, and the strength of your team often determines the size of your paycheck.

- **General Contractor:** Look for experience, references, and completed projects you can see with your own eyes.
- **Home Inspector:** Crucial before you buy—better to spend $500 upfront than $50,000 in missed problems later.
- **Realtor:** Choose one familiar with flips. They'll know which improvements bring the highest return in your market.
- **Attorney:** Contracts, permits, and zoning laws can sink a deal if ignored. An attorney protects your blind spots.

Mentor Insight: Treat your contractor like a partner, not a vendor. Respect their expertise, pay them on time, and maintain open communication. In return, you'll get priority treatment and smoother projects.

Step 4: Plan Your Timeline — Because Time = Money

Every extra week you hold the property costs you in taxes, utilities, and loan interest. Delays kill profits faster than anything else.

Your project timeline should include milestones for:

- Permits and approvals
- Demolition and repairs
- Inspections and city sign-offs
- Staging and photography
- Listing and marketing

Pro Tip

Use a simple project management tool like Trello, Asana, or even Google Sheets to track progress. When you treat your flip like a professional project, delays become visible before they turn into disasters.

Step 5: Managing the Rehab — Communication Is Currency

Renovations never go as planned. Walls hide surprises, contractors juggle other jobs, and supply chain issues can cause delays. Your best weapon? **Communicating ahead of time.**

- Conduct (or even twice-weekly) walkthroughs.
- Keep a detailed spreadsheet of all expenses.
- Document everything with photos.
- Address problems early rather than waiting for them to snowball.

Pro Secret

I once saved $7,000 on a project by catching a mistake in the plumbing layout during a walkthrough. Had I waited until the drywall was up, fixing it would have tripled the cost.

Step 6: Market and Stage for Maximum Appeal

You've put in the work. Now it's time to make buyers fall in love. The right marketing can add tens of thousands of dollars to your last sale.

- **Professional Photography:** Non-negotiable. Homes with professional photos sell faster and for more money.
- **Curb Appeal:** landscaping, fresh exterior paint, and a clean entryway set the tone. First impressions matter.
- **Neutral Staging:** Buyers need to picture themselves living there. Keep it light, clean, and inviting.

Luxury-Level Insight: I once staged a mid-tier home with a $1,500 staging budget. The result? We received multiple offers within a week, one of them $12,000 above asking. That's a return staging earns again and again.

Step 7: Negotiate the Sale — Protect Your Bottom Line

The irrevocable step is knowing when to stand firm and when to compromise.

- **Set Your Minimum:** Know your walk-away number before listing.
- **Use Your Realtor:** Let them handle the back-and-forth with buyers. They know when to push and when to close.
- **Don't Get Greedy:** A bird in the hand—a strong, qualified buyer—is often worth more than waiting for an extra $5,000.

Step 8: Legal & Inspection Must-Knows

Even after renovations, protect yourself:

- Always have a post-rehab inspection. Better to catch issues before your buyers do.
- Disclose every repair and update. Hiding problems leads to lawsuits.
- Understand zoning, permitting, and city regulations. Compliance is nonnegotiable.

Common Rookie Mistakes to Avoid

- Falling in love with a property before doing the math.
- Over-improving beyond neighborhood standards.
- Skipping inspections or rushing through permits.
- Underestimating carrying costs.
- Weak marketing stalls the sale.

Mentor Reminder: Flipping is not just about renovation skills—it's about **budgeting, project management, and market awareness.**

Case Study 1: The Starter Flip That Paid Off

Maria, a first-time investor, bought a two-bedroom bungalow in a rising neighborhood. The house needed only cosmetic upgrades: fresh paint, kitchen cabinets, updated lighting, and landscaping.

- Purchase Price: $95,000
- Renovations: $22,000
- Holding Costs: $4,500
- Selling Costs: $9,000

She managed her contractors, caught issues early, and stuck to her budget.

Result: The house sold for $165,000 in just four months. After all expenses, Maria cleared about $34,500 in profit.

Lesson: Start small. Cosmetic flips build experience without overwhelming risk.

Case Study 2: The Flip That Flopped

David, eager to "go big or go home," bought a fixer-upper for $210,000, hoping for a $60,000 profit. But he underestimated renovation costs and hired an unlicensed contractor.

- **Planned Renovations: $40,000**
- **Actual Renovations: $95,000**
- **Carrying Costs: $15,000**
- **Final Sale Price: $330,000**

Result: After all expenses, David earned just $2,000—a year of stress for almost no reward.

Lesson: Bigger is not always better. Without discipline, due diligence, and a skilled team, large flips can drain your wallet.

Why These Stories Matter?

Maria's success shows how discipline and planning create profit. David's cautionary tale reveals how enthusiasm without preparation destroys itself. Together, they underline one truth:

Smart flips are built on **strategy, not luck.**

Gentle Reflection

What's your biggest fear about flipping—overpaying, underestimating repairs, or mismanaging contractors?

Write it down. Then ask: *What system or team member could help me minimize this risk?*

When you face your fears with strategy, flipping transforms from a gamble into a legacy-building machine.

CHAPTER 8

Case Studies: Real Stories, Real Wins

In the last chapter, we explored the art of flipping properties and protecting yourself from rookie mistakes. Now, let's step into the real world and examine how actual investors — people just like you — navigated challenges, overcame setbacks, and turned their real estate ventures into wins worth celebrating.

Here's the truth: books and courses provide strategies, but **real-life stories reveal how those strategies play out in practice**. You'll see the highs, the lows, and the lessons that endure long after the deals are closed. These stories aren't about perfection — they're about persistence, discipline, and building legacies.

Whether you're considering your first rental, preparing for your first flip, or exploring short-term rentals, these case studies will do more than inspire you. They'll give you actionable takeaways and insights you can apply, ensuring you make confident, informed moves in your own journey.

Case Study 1: Jasmine — From Rental Rookie to Confident Investor

When Jasmine bought her first rental property for $180,000, she was juggling a full-time job and caring for her newborn baby. Like many first-time investors, she assumed real estate was about buying a home and collecting rent checks. She discovered it was far more complex.

Her first tenant turned out to be a nightmare: late payments, endless excuses, and property damage that cost thousands in repairs. At one point, Jasmine admitted she was ready to give up.

But instead of walking away, she shifted her perspective. Jasmine treated her rental like a **business** rather than a hobby. She began using digital tools like Zillow Rental Manager and TurboTenant to run thorough background and credit checks. She created a simple maintenance calendar and, most importantly, set aside a reserve fund for unexpected repairs.

Within two years, her property transformed from a constant headache into a reliable income stream. Today, Jasmine clears $1,200 per month in net rental income — and the property's equity has also appreciated, giving her long-term wealth alongside immediate cash flow.

"By checking and fixing things early, I saved money and avoided future stress. Now, I sleep better knowing my investment is protected." — Jasmine

Lessons Learned:

- Tenant screening is non-negotiable — it's your first line of defense.
- Budgeting for repairs upfront protects you from financial shocks later.
- Systems, not guesswork, allow a balance between real estate and personal life.

Mentor Insight: What Jasmine's story highlights is that **systems can manage stress**. Many investors fail not because the market is too harsh, but because disorganization drains them. By building processes early, she shifted from chaos to control. *Your wealth depends not only on financial returns but on peace of mind.*

Case Study 2: Marcus — Flipping Fast and Smart

Marcus loved the idea of flipping houses but kept falling into the same trap: underestimating costs and overestimating his free time. One early flip started at $150,000 but ballooned in repairs, with holding costs eating away at his expected profit. By the time he sold, his margin was almost gone.

Frustrated but determined, Marcus changed his approach for his next project. This time, he treated it like a business:

- He gathered multiple bids using Thumbtack and Angi, comparing not just price but contractor reliability.
- He built a detailed budget spreadsheet, adding a 20% contingency buffer.

- To protect his schedule, he hired a part-time project manager to keep contractors accountable.

The result? His next flip — a small ranch-style house — was completed in just 60 days and brought him a 17% profit margin, his best result yet.

"Flipping is about project management. Tight controls on both budget and timeline made all the difference." — Marcus

Lessons Learned:

- Multiple bids ensure quality and reduce risk.
- A contingency fund turns surprises into solvable issues.
- Accountability — either personal or outsourced — protects profits.

Mentor Insight: Marcus discovered the secret that separates amateurs from professionals: **discipline in numbers and accountability in execution**. A flip isn't a passion project — it's a financial engine. Treat every project as if you were preparing to open a luxury hotel: deadlines, budgets, and quality standards are sacred.

Case Study 3: Sara — The Airbnb Advantage

Sara, a teacher, wanted extra income but didn't want the hassle of long-term tenants. Instead, she explored short-term rentals. After running the numbers, she purchased a $220,000 townhouse near a tourist district.

Before committing, she used **AirDNA** to analyze occupancy rates and prices, ensuring profitability. She also confirmed the HOA and city rules to avoid costly mistakes that trap many first-time hosts.

Once listed on Airbnb and Vrbo, Sara treated her rental like a **hospitality brand**. She responded to guests, kept her property spotless, and even provided welcome baskets. The result? Glowing reviews, repeat bookings, and an income stream double what she would have earned from a traditional rental.

"Doing my homework and following the rules made all the difference. Short-term rentals became a powerful source of income once I treated them like a proper business." — Sara

Lessons Learned:

- Data tools are essential before purchase.
- Always confirm regulations before listing.
- Service and hospitality amplify profits.

Mentor Insight: Sara's success shows that short-term rentals are not just about property — they are about **experience design**. Numbers launch your venture, but service scales it. Every guest can become a marketing ambassador if you create delight. *You're not renting a unit — you're curating a legacy-worthy experience.*

Case Study 4: Daniel — The Duplex That Built Confidence

Daniel was cautious, worried about taking on too much risk. Instead of starting with a single-family rental, he bought a duplex, living in one unit while renting out the other.

This strategy, known as **house hacking**, covered most of his mortgage while still building equity. Within three years, Daniel saved enough to purchase his next property, all while keeping his risk low and his confidence high.

"At first, I was terrified of being a landlord. But living next door gave me peace of mind, and it turned out to be the best decision I've ever made." — Daniel.

Lessons Learned:

- House hacking lowers risk and speeds up learning.
- Living near tenants simplifies management.
- Starting small can snowball into larger wins.

Mentor Insight: Daniel's duplex is proof that **risk-adjusted entry builds legacies**. Wealth doesn't require massive leaps — it requires strategic footholds. By lowering exposure, he gained the confidence to scale. *Start where caution meets opportunity and let cash flow fuel your next step.*

Case Study 5: Linda — Flipping in Retirement

Not every investor begins young. Linda, a retiree, wanted a purpose after leaving her corporate career. She partnered with her son to buy a small fixer-upper. Together, they spent weekends painting, replacing fixtures, landscaping, and refinishing hardwood floors.

Six months later, they sold the property for a $45,000 profit. More importantly, Linda discovered joy and connection through the project.

"Flipping gave me purpose after retirement. The profit was wonderful, but the joy of working with my son was priceless." — Linda

Lessons Learned:

- Real estate is not bound by age — anyone can start.
- Cosmetic upgrades alone can generate strong returns.
- Real estate wins can be both financial and personal.

Mentor Insight: Linda reminds us that **wealth is more than money**. Legacy is about the memories you create, not just the profits you count. She built financial gain and emotional fulfillment. Ask yourself: *What if your portfolio wasn't just a cash-flow machine, but a memory-making machine too?*

Why These Stories Matter?

These case studies are more than inspiration — they are proof. They show that real estate success is not about luck or perfection, but about **discipline, strategy, and resilience**. Jasmine mastered systems. Marcus learned accountability. Sara built a brand. Daniel embraced the risk. Linda discovered the purpose.

Each story reveals a blueprint you can adapt to your journey. That is the power of legacy investing: it's not about copying someone else, but about tailoring timeless strategies to your life.

Gentle Reflection

Which story resonated with you most? Jasmine balancing motherhood and rentals? Marcus turning chaos into disciplined flipping? Is Sara building a hospitality-driven income? Daniel finding courage in house hacking? Or is Linda redefining retirement with purpose and profit?

Now, imagine your own future case study. One year from today, what story do you want to be telling? Please write it down. The first step to building your legacy is to define it.

Chapter 9

Resources, Tools & Checklists

In real estate, knowledge is leverage, and the right tools transform complexity into clarity. The difference between struggling through deals and moving like a seasoned pro often comes down to **systems**. Wealthy investors don't start from scratch; they use existing tools, checklists, and technology to simplify things, make fewer mistakes, and earn more money.

Think of this chapter as your **private arsenal** — a curated library of websites, apps, and checklists chosen not just for convenience, but for effectiveness. These are the same categories of tools high-performing investors use when scaling their portfolios into multi-million-dollar enterprises.

Your journey in real estate is not about collecting random tools; it's about **building an integrated system** that saves time, reduces risk, and gives you confidence in every decision.

Essential Websites & Platforms

MLS (Multiple Listing Service)

The MLS is the gold standard. It's the most accurate, up-to-date source for property listings, price changes, and market activity. While the public cannot access it, your realtor can — and therefore partnering with the right realtor matters.

Imagine this: you want a duplex under $300K in a specific zip code. Instead of spending hours on Zillow or Realtor.com, your realtor programs MLS alerts, and you're among the first to know when that property hits the market. Early access can mean the difference between securing a deal and losing it to a faster buyer.

Mentor Insight: Speed matters. The MLS doesn't just show what's available — it puts you at the front of the line.

Zillow & Realtor.com

These platforms are fantastic for browsing homes, scoping neighborhoods, and gauging trends. Think of them as **window shopping**. But remember: not all data here is accurate or updated in real-time. Use them for reconnaissance, then confirm with MLS data.

AirDNA

Considering short-term rentals? AirDNA provides detailed analytics on occupancy rates, average daily rates, and projected revenue. It's like having an X-ray of the Airbnb market before you spend a dollar.

Mashvisor

If you're torn between long-term rentals and short-term rentals, Mashvisor runs side-by-side comparisons. It doesn't just give you numbers — it clarifies strategy.

Rentometer

A quick way to benchmark rental prices in a neighborhood. If you plan to charge $2,000 in rent but the local average is $1,500, Rentometer alerts you before tenants do.

TurboTenant & Zillow Rental Manager

Both platforms streamline tenant placement by offering credit checks, background screenings, and lease templates. They save you from one of the most common (and costly) mistakes — placing the wrong tenant.

Thumbtack, HomeAdvisor, Angi

Finding reliable contractors is half the battle. These sites give you access to vetted professionals with reviews, ratings, and even photos of past work. Use them not just to save money, but to safeguard quality.

Mentor Insight: A property's value is not just in its walls — it's in the professionals you trust to repair, improve, and protect those walls.

Credit Karma and AnnualCreditReport.com

Every real estate journey starts with financing, and financing begins with credit. These free platforms allow you to monitor, repair, and track your credit health. A slight improvement in your credit score can mean tens of thousands of dollars in interest saved over the life of a loan.

Must-Have Apps for Investors

Your phone can either distract you or make you money. For investors who want leverage, these apps belong on your home screen:

- **DealCheck:** analyze properties for ROI, cap rate, and payback period. Enter the property's details and know within minutes whether it's worth pursuing.
- **BiggerPockets:** More than an app — it's a global community. Ask questions, connect with mentors, or run calculators that professionals use daily. Their podcasts and forums alone can replace years of trial and error.
- **PropertyFixer:** Tailored for flippers. It estimates rehab costs and resale values to prevent the #1 flipper mistake: underestimating expenses.
- **Google Keep / Evernote:** Think of them as your mobile filing cabinets. Keep inspection notes, receipts, and photos organized.

- **Expensify:** Taxes become simple when expenses are tracked in real time. Snap a photo of a receipt, and it's stored for later reporting.

Mentor Insight: High-level investors don't just rely on memory. They rely on data. Every receipt, every note, every inspection — logged, stored, retrievable. This is how you scale like a professional.

Primary Checklists to Keep You on Track

Checklists are the invisible armor of elite investors. They prevent oversight, save money, and bring clarity when emotions are high.

Pre-Purchase Checklist

- Define your investment goals (cash flow, appreciation, or both?).
- Get pre-approved for financing.
- Research neighborhoods, schools, and amenities.
- Order a professional inspection.
- Request an appraisal.
- Verify property permits and legal status.

Luxury Reminder: Discipline at this stage prevents $50,000 mistakes later.

Rental Management Checklist

- Screen tenants with credit, background, and references.
- Prepare clear lease agreements.
- Collect security deposits.
- Schedule routine maintenance and annual inspections.
- Track all income/expenses with software.
- Stay compliant with landlord-tenant laws.

Mentor Insight: Treat rentals like a business, not a hobby. Businesses thrive on systems, not good intentions.

Flip Project Checklist

- Build a detailed budget and timeline.
- Get three contractor bids.
- Secure permits before work begins.
- Monitor progress with check-ins.
- Stage property before listing.
- Market with professional photography.
- Add a 15–20% contingency buffer.

Bonus Checklists for Real-Life Scenarios

Because elite investors prepare for every stage, here are bonus checklists to elevate your execution.

Closing Day Checklist (Buyers)

- Bring ID and required documents.
- Review closing disclosure.
- Double-check the down payment and closing costs.
- Do one last property walkthrough.
- Collect keys, garage openers, and codes.
- Store paperwork.

Move-In Checklist (Landlords)

- Document, property condition with photos.
- Provide tenants with keys and emergency contacts.
- Review the lease agreement together.
- Test appliances and safety systems.
- Collect the signed move-in checklist.
- Share house rules.

Quarterly Maintenance Checklist

- Test smoke and CO detectors.
- Replace HVAC filters.
- Inspect the plumbing for leaks.
- Check the roof and gutters.
- Walk the exterior for cracks/damage.
- Service appliances.

Pro move: A $20 HVAC filter can save you from a $5,000 replacement later.

Gentle Reflection

Which tool or checklist feels most relevant to your next step? Perhaps it's downloading DealCheck, running your first Rentometer report, or preparing a move-in checklist for your next tenant.

Start small, stay consistent, and remember **systems build wealth as much as properties do.** Each tool here is not just about saving time — it's about elevating you from an investor into a **legacy builder.**

CHAPTER 10

The Mindset of a Successful Real Estate Investor

I n real estate, the most powerful asset you own isn't a property. This isn't a bank account. Your network isn't even involved. It's your **mindset**.

Everything else — the spreadsheets, checklists, contractors, and capital — flows from this. If your thinking is limited, your results will always be capped. If your mindset is expansive, resilient, and strategic, you can weather any storm and multiply opportunities others don't even see.

Think about it: the same market crash that wipes out one investor can create generational wealth for another. The difference? No luck, not timing — **mindset.**

This chapter is about mastering the **inner game of real estate**. Because high-level investors don't just buy property; they shape futures, build legacies, and move with the confidence of people who know that success isn't random — it's designed.

Be open to learning and improving

Luxury-level investors view every setback as **a tuition payment for mastery.** They don't avoid mistakes; they alchemize them into strategy.

Emily is a perfect example. On her first flip, she miscalculated repair costs and lost $5,000. A rookie would have quit. Emily didn't. Instead, she joined a local investors' group, sought mentorship, and built a vetted contractor network. Two years later, she was running profitable flips like clockwork.

Luxury Lesson: Failures are not walls; they are doors. The cost may sting, but what you gain is equity in wisdom.

Action Step: Write one "failure" from your financial or personal life. Next to it, record the lesson it taught you. This reframing transforms scars into stepping stones.

Keep Calm and Carry On

Real estate rewards patience as much as persistence. Deals collapse. Financing stalls. Tenants walk away. The impatient retreat; the disciplined advance.

Carlos made 12 offers before he closed on his first rental property. Twelve. Most beginners would have stopped at five. Carlos didn't. That persistence now funds his life through four rental properties, producing steady cash flow.

Luxury Lesson: Every "no" isn't rejection — it's redirection toward the deal that was designed for you.

Action Step: Set a non-negotiable goal for offers each month. Reframe each rejection as a rehearsal for the "yes" that matters.

Stay curious and keep learning

The real estate landscape is alive. Markets shift. Regulations strengthen. Technology speeds up. The investor who keeps learning stays ahead; the one who doesn't, falls behind.

Sara, an Airbnb host, could have settled for decent results. Instead, she studied forums, analyzed top-performing hosts, and invested in professional photography and automated systems. Within a year, her revenue doubled — not because she owned more property, but because she expanded her knowledge.

Luxury Lesson: Knowledge compounds just like capital. Each insight is an investment that multiplies your returns.

Action Step: Dedicate at least 20 minutes daily to feeding your mind. Podcasts, articles, mastermind groups — treat this as non-negotiable mental conditioning.

Manage Fear and Risk

Fear doesn't vanish with success; it strengthens. The difference between amateur and authority is how you respond to it.

John was terrified of buying his first duplex. He saw tenants defaulting, roofs collapsing, repairs spiraling out of control. Instead of freezing, he created a contingency budget, set aside three months of reserves, and tightened his tenant screening process. That property has been cash-flowing for three years.

Luxury Lesson: Fear is energy. Channel it into preparation, and it becomes your sharpest strategic edge.

Action Step: Make a "risk list" for your next deal. For each risk, outline one protective action. When fear is named, it loses power.

Visualize Success

Top athletes and CEOs use visualization not as fantasy, but as **performance architecture**. Investors should too.

Maya wanted to replace her 9- to–5 income with real estate. She built a vision board filled with rental properties, travel photos, and debt-free living. Every morning, she anchored herself in this vision. Within five years, she achieved it — $7,000 in passive income.

Luxury Lesson: Visualization is not dreaming — it is rehearsing success so that your actions fall into alignment.

Action Step: Write your five-year real estate vision. Number of properties. Cash flow. Lifestyle shifts. Place it somewhere visible — revisit it daily.

Cultivate Resilience

Every investor falls. The elite refuse to stay down.

Marcus lost almost everything in the 2008 crash. Many peers abandoned real estate forever. Marcus dissected his mistakes — over-leveraging — and rebuilt smarter. Today, he owns a portfolio stronger than ever and mentors others to avoid his past missteps.

Luxury Lesson: Wealth is built not in the absence of setbacks, but in the relentless resilience to rise after each one.

Action Step: Start a "bounce-back journal." Document setbacks, emotions, and lessons. Over time, this archive becomes your personal blueprint for resilience.

Pro Secret: Community is Currency

The wealthiest investors don't operate alone. They build inner circles of mentors, peers, and advisors who elevate their strategy and sharpen their resilience.

When markets shift, or challenges arise, this network becomes the ultimate safety net — and springboard. Success at the highest level, is never solitary.

High-Performance Investor Mindset Checklist

Daily Habits

- Revisit your **vision statement** and visualize your future portfolio.
- Spend at least **20 minutes learning** (podcasts, articles, books, forums).
- Record one **gratitude + one growth lesson** from the day.
- Review your financial dashboard — even if it's simple at first. Awareness builds mastery.

Habits

- Analyze at least **3–5 deals**, to sharpen evaluation skills.
- Connect with your network — mentor, peer, or group — and exchange insights.
- Journal one "setback" or challenge and reframe it into a **Luxury Lesson**.
- Adjust your short-term action plan in alignment with your five-year vision.

Habits

- Review your **risk list** and update contingency plans.
- Audit expenses, cash flow, and portfolio performance.
- Attend at least one **learning event** (webinar, meetup, or mastermind).
- Identify one limiting belief and replace it with an empowering one.

Gentle Reflection

- What mindset shift do you need to embrace right now to move forward?
- Are you allowing fear, impatience, or past mistakes to stall your growth?
- Which story — Emily's rebound, Carlos's persistence, Sara's curiosity, John's risk management, Maya's

vision, or Marcus's comeback — mirrors where you are today?

- Which **daily or habit** from the checklist will you commit to?

CHAPTER 11

Conclusion + Next Steps

You didn't just read a book—you made an investment in yourself, in your future, and in the legacy you're about to build. That alone sets you apart from the vast majority of people. Most individuals only daydream about financial freedom, whispering "someday." You, however, took action. You opened these pages, committed to learning, and stayed with me until the very end. That makes you a builder of futures, not just a consumer of information.

But let's get clear about one thing: knowledge alone won't change your life. You could have the sharpest spreadsheets, the most detailed checklists, and even insider strategies—but if you don't *act*, nothing shifts. The divide between dreamers and doers is courage. It's courage to pick up the phone and call a lender, courage to make that first offer, courage to manage that first tenant, courage to trust yourself enough to move forward.

Every empire begins with a single brick. The property you research today, the offer you submit tomorrow, or the renovation you start this month—these minor acts, stacked together, form the foundation of a dynasty.

Now Is Your Moment

- **No more "someday."** Real estate rewards those who act with purpose *today*, not tomorrow.
- **No more analysis paralysis.** You've studied the tools, strategies, and systems. Now, it's time to put them to work.
- **No more waiting for permission.** You don't need perfection to start—you only need momentum.

Action creates clarity. Clarity creates results.

The Best Investors Aren't Perfect— They're Persistent

Every investor you admire has battle scars. They've lost deals, endured setbacks, and doubted themselves. The difference between those who succeed and those who stall isn't intelligence or luck—it's persistence.

- It was uncomfortable when they showed up.
- Instead of quitting, they learned from their mistakes.
- Building continued, even when progress felt slow.

And now, you're in the same arena. By finishing this book, you've joined the rare circle of people who don't just talk about freedom—they pursue it.

Pro Secret
The market won't wait for you. Interest rates shift. Neighborhoods transform. Deals come and go. The winners

aren't those who know the most—they're the ones who *act* with confidence and consistency.

So, take the step. Even a small one. Especially a small one. Because momentum compounds faster than you think.

Your Legacy Starts Today

Here's a practical exercise I encourage you to complete *right now*:

- Write one action step you'll take in the next 7 days. (Example: "Schedule a call with a local realtor," "Review my credit report," or "Attend two open houses.")
- Say it out loud. There's power in verbalizing a commitment—it transforms intention into reality.
- Do it. No excuses. No delays.

Your empire won't rise overnight, but it will never rise at all if you don't lay that first brick.

From Investor to Real Estate CEO

Owning a property is one thing. Building a sustainable, wealth-generating enterprise is another. The shift from *individual investor* to *real estate CEO* is where true freedom, sustainability, and legacy wealth are created.

Here's how to make that leap:

- **Build Your Dream Team**: Stop trying to wear every hat. Assemble a team—agent, lender, contractor, property manager, attorney—who can operate without daily handholding. Your time should be spent leading, not micromanaging.
- **Systematize Everything**: Leverage tools for tenant screening, online rent collection, automated maintenance requests, and project management. The more you automate, the more scalable your empire becomes.
- **Track the Numbers**: Monitor ROI, cash flow, debt-service coverage, and vacancy rates. Numbers don't lie—they keep your emotions in check and your strategy sharp.
- **Set Bold Growth Targets**: Don't drift—design. Set quarterly and yearly goals like "acquire one new rental per quarter" or "increase net cash flow by 20%." Treat your portfolio with the same discipline Fortune 500 companies treat their P&Ls.
- **Lead With Vision**: Are you aiming for financial independence, early retirement, or leaving a legacy for your family? Keep the "why" front and center—it's your compass.

The realistic goal isn't just to own doors. The goal is to craft a life where your money works harder than you do, where your investments fund your freedom, and where your family thrives because of the foundation you laid.

A Gentle Push Forward

Ask yourself right now:

- What's the *first small win* I can claim this week?
- Who is the one person I need to connect with to advance my goals?
- How will I celebrate progress—even if it's just one step forward?

Remember, your real estate journey doesn't end here. This isn't the final chapter—it's the prologue to your own story.

So take the step. Write that offer. Call that lender. Walk that property.

One day, you'll look back and realize that this was the exact moment your true story began—the chapter where knowledge turned into action, and dreams began transforming into your empire.

Luxury Closing Note: You're not just an investor now—you are a visionary, a builder, a legacy creator. The decisions you make today echo into the future, shaping not just your finances but your family's freedom for generations. This is bigger than property. This is your empire. Build it.

Appendix & References

Glossary of Key Real Estate Terms

- Appraisal: an expert's estimate of a property's value.
- Cap Rate: A ratio used to estimate the return on an investment property.
- Closing Costs: Fees and expenses paid at the closing of a real estate transaction.
- Contingency: conditions that must be met for a real estate contract to be binding.
- Equity: the value of ownership in a property, calculated as market value minus any debts.
- Loan-to-Value (LTV): The ratio of the loan amount to the appraised property value.
- PMI (Private Mortgage Insurance): Insurance that protects the lender if the borrower defaults, often required for down payments under 20%.
- REIT (Real Estate Investment Trust): A company that owns or finances income-producing real estate.
- ARV (After Repair Value): The estimated value of a property after renovation.

Recommended Reading & Resources

- Books:
  - ○ The Millionaire Real Estate Investor by Gary Keller
  - ○ Rich Dad Poor Dad by Robert Kiyosaki
  - ○ The Book on Rental Property Investing by Brandon Turner

- Websites:
  - ○ BiggerPockets: Comprehensive real estate investing community and education.
  - ○ Zillow: property listings and market trends.
  - ○ Realtor.com: Reliable property search and guides.
  - ○ AirDNA: short-term rental market analytics.
  - ○ HUD.gov: Housing and Urban Development resources.

- Apps:
  - ○ DealCheck (deal analysis)
  - ○ TurboTenant (tenant screening)
  - ○ Mashvisor (investment property data)

Useful Checklists & Worksheets

- Pre-Purchase Checklist
- Flip Budget Spreadsheet Template
- Tenant Screening Checklist
- Rental Property Maintenance Schedule
- Negotiation Prep Worksheet

Contact hello@bookedandbrandedpublishing.com to request editable versions of these resources.

References & Data Sources

- National Association of Realtors (NAR) Market Reports
- U.S. Census Bureau Housing Data
- Freddie Mac & Fannie Mae Loan Programs
- Local MLS Data & Real Estate Boards
- AirDNA Short-Term Rental Reports

Disclaimer

This book is intended for informational purposes only and does not constitute financial, legal, or investment advice. Readers should consult qualified professionals before making real estate decisions.

Thank you for your purchase. I'd appreciate it if you could write a short Amazon review, assuming this book has been helpful. Your words help others find this message and remind them they are not alone.

where hustle meets strategy

Work With Me

If you want to skip costly mistakes, fast-track your investment success, and build wealth with confidence, you've come to the right place.

With over a decade of hands-on real estate investing and a strategic business consultant background — plus an MBA focused on entrepreneurship — I bring the savvy and real-world experience you need to win.

I work only with a select group of motivated investors each quarter to ensure personalized attention and maximum results.

How can I support you?

Whether you're a first-time buyer, rental property owner, or flipper, my coaching and mentorship will help you:

- Identify and seize the best deals
- Navigate financing and negotiation with ease
- Manage properties and teams
- Build a sustainable, profitable real estate portfolio
- Cultivate the mindset and habits for long-term success

Limited-Time Bonus

Book your free consultation this month and receive my exclusive Real Estate Success Starter Kit — a toolkit packed with templates, checklists, and insider tips to speed up your journey.

What Clients Say

"Stephanie's coaching saved me thousands and gave me the confidence to close my first rental property. Her insights are practical, clear, and motivating." — Jasmine B.

"Working with Stephanie helped me streamline my flip projects and increase my profits. She's a significant change." — Marcus T.

Ready to Work Together?

Visit www.bookedandbrandedpublishing.com/coaching or email me at hello@bookedandbrandedpublishing.com to schedule your free consultation and start building your empire.

Where hustle meets strategy.

About the Author

Stephanie Williams is an entrepreneur, strategic business consultant, and seasoned real estate investor and mentor with over a decade of experience building wealth through personal properties, rentals, Airbnb, and flips. She holds an MBA with a focus on entrepreneurship and combines hands-on investing knowledge with business strategy to empower others on their real estate journeys.

Stephanie's mission is to help new and experienced investors simplify the complex world of real estate and achieve financial freedom with confidence and clarity.

Where hustle meets strategy.

Thank you for reading. We've included a free downloadable workbook to help you apply these principles.
Scan for FREE WORKBOOK printable tracker & digital copy